EVOLUTION OF TRADITIONAL ARCHITECTURE

In the Deep South

Architecture had humble origins in the wild native lands of deep southern America. Ship timbers and rough hewn cypress boards were used to make trappers' cabins and simple homes for Acadians. These so-called "Cajuns" (a corruption of Acadian) were forced to leave Nova Scotia because they refused to pledge their allegiance to the King of England. At roughly the same time, Creole planters from France and Spain, and people of English descent who migrated from the eastern seaboard states arrived in the area.

Large numbers of Cajuns settled in the bayou country of Louisiana and Mississippi and began to build their typical cabins. They were plain little boxes with a gabled roof covered with shingles, and vertical boards covering the outside walls. There was always an open staircase on the front porch, and it led to the attic. The Cajuns lived off the land, hunting and fishing, raising vegetables and spices, some of which were introduced by the Indians and the Afro-Americans.

The early bricks that were made for the Creoles on the Mississippi Coast and in New Orleans were sandy and soft. Mortar was made from the lime in clam shells. Builders learned to coat the walls with plaster to prevent their deterioration from the dampness. Eventually, thick hard bricks of clay were formed and baked by the slaves, who contributed so much to these historic homes. With that innovation, larger and sturdier homes could be built. Planters who had first settled in the West Indies, and then came up the Mississippi River, often in their own ships, knew about building raised houses with umbrella like roofs which shaded wide galleries built outside the walls of the homes.

Plantation owners became wealthy almost overnight as cotton crops were translated into gold. Adventurous English people from the east coast brought Federal, Queen Anne, and Georgian influences to the architecture. They also introduced interior decoration that featured Adam mantles and interior wood trim employing straight lines and graceful carved garlands. At the height of the Antebellum (pre Civil War) period, Classical Greek Architecture was adopted throughout the area as the mark of the wealthy planter.

The earlier homes were more modest and used the tasteful columns, with plain capitals at the top, of the Doric order, the oldest and simplest of the three Greek orders. Next the ornamental scrolls of the Ionic capitals, often resting on fluted columns, were stylishly displayed across the front of the grander homes. Finally, the elaborate Corinthian columns adorned the largest mansions, with Acanthus leaves surrounding the tall capitals. This order was surely the ultimate in grandeur for the mansions that were built just as the war clouds were gathering. Here and there, a few exotic touches appeared: a Romanesque influence displayed deep red brick with uncluttered white trim; a flared capital borrowed from Egypt appeared on a column, with the fluting extending to the top of the column and up through the capital; or a Moorish arch was adopted from the so-called Islamic Revival.

Last of all, at the end of the 19th Century, new facades came on the scene, that were laughingly called "American Architecture." The Victorian houses were built with steep roofs that came to a peak, as acute as an inverted V. There were gables, and turrets, spires and flying buttresses - effects growing out of the Gothic Revival Architecture. Mark Twain blamed the fad on Sir Walter Scott's historic novel, "Ivanhoe." All parts of the house, especially the galleries and porches, were adorned with fanciful, jigsawed ornamentation, which we now refer to as "gingerbread." People still laugh a bit, but these homes are being bought and restored today by loving owners. Some are as decorative and luscious as a birthday cake, so we say, "Each to his own." Pick your favorite period of architecture and enjoy.

CAJUN CABIN

St. Martinville • Louisiana

This is a reconstruction of the very early Cajun Cabins that were built by the Acadians that came to the swamps, wet prairies, and coast lands of south Louisiana and south Mississippi. The cabin had either one or two doors in the front of the house, and the usual outside stairway or ladder that led to the loft. The boys of the family slept up there. Since dry land was scarce, they were often built fairly close to each other. There was a pot shelf outside the kitchen window, so "Maman" could wash dishes in the dish pan placed upon it, and gossip with the neighbor at the same time. This cabin now houses an outlet for Acadian crafts. *Located in Longfellow-Evangeline State Park, St. Martinville, Louisiana.*

DOG TROT HOUSE

Baton Rouge • Louisiana

The so-called "Dog Trot" house, is one of the earliest styles of construction to be found. The few remaining dog trot houses are found in north Louisiana and north Mississippi. They usually have the kitchen and dining room on one side of the house and the bedrooms on the other side. The accommodating space between the two sides allows for greater air circulation on hot afternoons and is the forerunner of the screened breezeway in more modern houses. The name, of course, comes from the fact that the family dog could trot up and down through the center. We can imagine family members, on a hot afternoon, sitting in rocking chairs, catching the draft. A couple of hounds would probably have been there with them, lying alongside the family, thumping their tails on the wooden floor when spoken to.

TRAPPER'S CABIN

Baton Rouge • Louisiana

Looking out from under the eaves, we can see the back of a trapper's cabin nearby. The chimney is of bousillage construction, (pronounced boo-see-yazh), and meaning botched or bungled. It was used by the French people to build a simple but serviceable chimney. Small cross sticks were placed two by two at each level, as if one were building a log cabin. As the construction of the chimney went up, wet clay was packed all around the branches, and when the whole fabrication dried hard, the structure was a good substitute for bricks and mortar. Often, for the sake of safety, the chimney had to be rebuilt from time to time. The cabin itself is built of wide slabs of cypress, rather than logs.

ACADIAN VILLAGE

Lafayette • Louisiana

The great Exodus of the Acadians occurred in 1755. Several of the houses which they built in the "wet prairies," as the marshes were called, have been saved by being moved to Acadian Village in Lafayette, Louisiana. The collection forms an extremely authentic replica of a village of the second half of the 19th century. The houses have been placed along both sides of a sleepy little bayou and a small white church and a store are included. This particular house was built by Dorsene Castille at Pont-Breaux, Louisiana in about 1860. It is a little more stylish than the early cabins, and is called La Maison Castille. *The Acadian Village, Chemin Ridge Road, Lafayette, Louisiana.*

FLOREWOOD RIVER PLANTATION

Greenwood • Mississippi

Florewood is a reconstruction of what a former River Plantation in Mississippi would have looked like. It is beautifully done and is typical of the frame construction of plantation buildings in north Mississippi. The lines of the buildings are simple, but the restoration is exceedingly complete and authentic, particularly in regard to the primitive furniture in the outbuildings. It is a state park and offers traditional museum displays and living history presentations of activities carried on at a large cotton plantation in the lifestyle of the time before the Civil War. *Located on US 82, 2 miles west of Greenwood, Mississippi.*

MOUNT LOCUST INN

Natchez • Mississippi

Inns and taverns were often the first buildings to be constructed in newly opened up territories. Mount Locust Inn is one of these, and is located at the southern end of the Natchez Trace. It rests on a small hill, just above the level of the Trace and is properly called a "stand," as the early inns on the trace were referred to as stands. They were often run by persons of mixed French and Native American ancestry. Their simple beds were a boon to travelers using this long and dangerous route from Nashville to Natchez. *Located just north of Natchez on the Natchez Trace (off US 61).*

KING'S TAVERN

Natchez • Mississippi • 1770

King's Tavern is the oldest building in Natchez. As the frontier advanced from the East to the West, and up the Mississippi River, the most welcome buildings were the taverns, where travelers could spend the night, have a meal, and quaff a pint of ale. They were often built of ship timber, as this one is, on a brick foundation one room high. The wooden second story was held together with wooden pegs, forced through the huge timbers. The ground floor housed the kitchen, storage rooms, and dining area, and the travelers slept in the upstairs rooms, often several to a bed if foot traffic through the area was heavy.

HOPE FARM

Natchez • Mississippi • 1775

Hope Farm is a gracious house which was added to in later years. The present wing of the home was the original part of this comfortable farm house, and the large front part is the addition that was made in 1789. This was never intended to be an aristocratic house, for it was built before the large cotton fortunes were made, but it is a sturdy house, built of cypress timbers, and its design for easy living is obvious. There are galleries in both the front and the back, and a small one runs along the rear wing. These two parts of the building frame a lovely enclosed garden at the rear.

THE ACADIAN HOUSE

St. Martinville • Louisiana • 1780

In Longfellow-Evangeline State Park, there is a fine example of an Acadian house. Built by the widow of a French military officer, it is a sizeable stalwart house, much more than a mere cabin, but typical of the construction of the time. The structural timbers were fastened with wooden pegs and the first floor walls, of handmade brick, are 14 inches thick. The upper walls are made of bousillage, which is a mud and moss mixture placed between the cypress beams. The house is now furnished as a museum. Legend had it that this was the home of Louis Arceneaux who was the Gabriel of Longfellow's poem "Evangeline." *Located in Longfellow-Evangeline State Park, St. Martinville, Louisiana.*

DESTREHAN MANOR

Destrehan • Louisiana • 1787

Destrehan Manor is the oldest plantation home left intact in the lower Mississippi Valley. It shows the influence of the West Indies, which is typical of the early planter's homes, since many of the planters had lived on plantations there before coming to Louisiana. The main floor was raised and became the living area. The roof was tall and wide, to give shade and to keep the house cool. The window sashes opened high, making doorways to let the breezes blow through, but the louvred blinds (called jalousies) could be closed at certain times of the day to keep out the hot sun. The ground floor became the working area. *Located on the River Road near the town of Destrehan, Louisiana.*

SPRINGFIELD

Fayette • Mississippi • 1790

Springfield is a rather plain two story house, built entirely of brick made on the plantation, as was often the case in these early homes. However, the front facade is graced by galleries on both levels and simple white Doric columns. It shows the influence of architecture from the eastern seaboard states. The interior rooms of the house are spacious, and intricate designs in the Federal style of Adams have been added to the mantels and the woodwork. The builder was a colonel under General Andrew Jackson, and the home's claim to fame is that Jackson was married here to Rachel Robards in 1791. Sitting on the upstairs gallery and catching the cool breezes was a lovely way to spend an evening. *Located on Hwy 553, West of Fayette, Mississippi.*

MAGNOLIA MOUND

Baton Rouge • Louisiana • 1791

Magnolia Mound was built on a high natural ridge, situated in a grove of large, old live oak and magnolia trees. It was built by a German planter who never meant it to be an elaborate showcase of a house. It is pure of line and devoid of frill and pretense, but it is a very practical and liveable early southern plantation home. The thick plank floors are still in excellent condition. Reconstructions of an overseer's house and an outdoor kitchen have been added to the grounds. *Located on Nicholson Drive in downtown Baton Rouge, Louisiana.*

THE COTTAGE

St. Francisville • Louisiana • 1795 • 1859

The Cottage was built in the heart of English Louisiana which is in the toe of this boot-shaped state. It shows none of the grandeur of later homes, but is an ideally spacious country house. The main structure was periodically added to, and that accounts for the dates. The additions were so well planned, that the entire pleasing structure seems to have been designed at the same time. The building appears low because of the overhanging roof, but there is a second story with dormer windows. Several of the original outbuildings remain. *Located just north of St. Francisville on US 61.*

KENT HOUSE

Alexandria • Louisiana • 1796

The central section of this house is of "bousillage" construction, which marks it as a very early house. Bousillage was a way of building with beams (usually cypress), and packing a mixture of mud and moss in between the wood frame. The wings at either side were added later, but all three sections are raised above the ground floor on high piers of slave made bricks. Despite the simplicity of the house, the interior has great style. Outbulidings have been added to the rear of the house, to complete the complex of a typical plantation in the heartland of Louisiana. *Located on Bayou Rapides Road in Alexandria.*

THE HOUSE ON ELLICOTT HILL

Natchez • Mississippi • 1798

This building sitting atop Ellicott Hill, overlooking the river traffic on the Mississippi, has been called Connelly's Tavern in the past, and was an early landmark. Andrew Ellicott, in defiance of Spain, raised the American Flag on this hill in 1797. The house was built in the prevailing style of Spanish Provincial architecture. A fine view of the river may be had from both galleries, standing high above the pedestrian traffic below. The roof and upper gallery are both supported by nine colonettes, and an exterior staircase connects the two.

LINDEN

Natchez • Mississippi • 1800

Linden is a gracious, inviting home. The central portion of the house is actually a little earlier than 1800. The original width was expanded and two wings were added later to the back of the house to form ells with the main structure. The original part was a two story building constructed of cypress, fastened together with wooden pegs. The gallery, graced by pure Doric columns, was built across the length of the house, and a charming portico was added to the second level, where a balustrade continues around the entire gallery. An oval window in the triangle of the pediment and a fanlight window over the front door add a certain grandeur to the house.

OAKLEY

St. Francisville • Louisiana • 1808

Oakley is one of the more simply constructed early houses, but is more monumental than some, in that it has two stories built over a brick basement, giving it a total of three stories, an unusual height. It makes extensive use of the galleries, by shading the upper one totally and the lower one partially with louvred blinds, which were often called jalousies in the French south. A wide exterior staircase leads to the main floor and a narrower one to the second. Oakley is particularly famous because John James Audubon, the famous painter of birds, lived here at one time, and taught various fine arts to the young people. *Located on LA 965, east of St. Francisville.*

ROSEMONT

Woodville • Mississippi • 1810

Famous for being the boyhood home of Jefferson Davis, President of the Confederacy during the War Between the States, Rosemont is a Federal style cottage. It is an inviting dwelling, and was built by his parents, Samuel and Jane Davis. The central hall with large doors front and back which can be opened wide, acts as a breezeway, and opens onto the back porch, where the family could look down into a wooded ravine. These early homes were always built for great comfort. *Located in Woodville, Mississippi, just off US 61 on MS 24.*

HERMITAGE

Darrow • Louisiana • 1812

Originally called L'Hermitage, because it was built for the French Colomb family, Hermitage is one of the fine early houses, and its very simplicity makes it handsome. It looks larger than it really is, because the columns encircle the galleries of the central structure, but as in all the earlier houses, the rooms are smaller and the ceiling is lower than in later homes. This is one of the earliest of the pure classical Greek houses, and with its profusion of Doric columns of perfect proportion, and an entablature above them with a detail of dentation, it resembles a miniature Greek temple. *Located on LA 75 near Darrow, Louisiana.*

AUBURN

Natchez • Mississippi • 1812

Just before dusk, Auburn takes on a special glow, a reflection of the setting sun on its soft pink brick. It is the centerpiece of Duncan Park and was a gift to the City of Natchez from the heirs of the last Duncan owner. The front entrance is graced by a grand two story portico supported by tall Ionic columns. The second level of the balcony is guarded by a balustrade with delicately carved spindles, and both upstairs and downstairs entrances are graced with elegant fanlights. Its most unique feature is a spiral free standing staircase in the front hall. This house is typical of a more sophisticated style of Greek architecture. *Located in Natchez, Mississippi at Duncan Park.*

MONMOUTH

Natchez • Mississippi • 1818

A pristine white house that often looks pale pink when the sunlight is soft and rosy, Monmouth is a grand place. It definitely was built in the style of Greek architecture, but the columns that support the extremely large portico are square and the balustrade of the second floor gallery is designed in a motif of diagonals. The carving of the interior woodwork is a holdover from the Federal style of Adams. This enormous home is a monument to General Quitman of Mexican War fame, as it crowns one of the highest hills in Natchez.

FRANCES PLANTATION

Franklin • Louisiana • 1820

We again see the West Indian influence in this house, as we have in many of the early plantations homes. It is typical of the early Louisiana houses, and is graced by beautiful upper and lower galleries. It faces the Historic Spanish Trail in the front, and scenic Bayou Teche runs by the back yard as it meanders toward the Gulf of Mexico. The lower portion of the house was fashioned of handmade brick, laid in a herringbone design, and the upper part was built of Louisiana red cypress. *Located three miles east of Franklin, Louisiana on old US 90, now LA 182.*

ROSALIE

Natchez • Mississippi • 1820

Rosalie has been restored and cared for by the Mississippi Daughters of the American Revolution. This renowned two-story house was constructed entirely of red brick, over a raised basement. One is introduced to the house by entering through a magnificent tetrastyle portico, the same height as the roof. The columns still maintain the early Doric pattern, and the roof is crowned by a belvedere, enclosed in a white wooden guard rail. These belvederes were useful for watching the river boats, or to see if the show boat was nearing the landing at Natchez.

McRAVEN

Vicksburg • Mississippi • 1825 • 1849

One of the most delicate facades in Vicksburg belongs to McRaven. The intricately designed double columns are unique, and even the balustrade between the columns on the second floor gallery is finely detailed with exceptionally thin posts supporting the rail. The interior of the house takes one on a journey through time, because it was constructed in three different periods: 1825, 1836, and 1849. It began as a frontier cottage, to which Greek Revival rooms were added, and was finally given the front addition of a Philadelphia townhouse, still showing the Classical style, but with an Italianate influence.

THE MYRTLES

St. Francisville • Louisiana • 1830

This is an example of one of the early grander houses, with a front gallery that runs the length of the house. It was built on an early Spanish land grant. Set in a grove of live oaks and crepe myrtles, the house has a sense of elegance because the exceptionally long gallery is framed all around with lacy wrought iron work. This shows the same Spanish influence as the galleries in the New Orleans French Quarter. The interior of the home exhibits the early use of decorative plaster interior trim in moldings and center medallions. *Located north of St. Francisville on US 61.*

SHADOWS-ON-THE-TECHE

New Iberia • Louisiana • 1831

Shadows-on-the-Teche was built in the favorite Greek Revival style of the period, but with the red bricks left to show their color, so it does not have the "white temple" look. Although the builder was of English descent, he chose some of the influence of the French Cajun area in which he lived, with the outside stairways, and the jalousies (louvred panels) protecting them from the elements. The house was restored during the 1920's by Weeks Hall, the great-grandson of the builder, who was often called "the last of the southern gentleman." The Shadows is now owned and maintained by the National Trust for Historic Preservation. *Located on Bayou Teche in New Iberia.*

ASPHODEL

Jackson • Louisiana • 1833

Asphodel exhibits the Doric style, the earliest of Classic Greek architecture, which gives it a very pure look without any frivolous embellishments. The eight columns across the center are connected by a graceful balustrade. The two wings blend beautifully with the main house, which hugs the crest of a hill, surrounded by azaleas and trailing ivy. The wings appear almost as miniature houses added on the two sides of the central building. This gives the house a sort of small doll house look, but it is actually quite spacious inside. The name comes from classic literature and refers to daffodils and narcissus. *Located twenty five miles north of Baton Rouge, off US 61.*

ROSEWOOD MANOR

Columbus • Mississippi • 1835

This is one of the oldest homes in Columbus. The detailing around the doors and windows was done in the style of the Federal Period of architecture, which was brought to Mississippi from the East coast, and we are told that the outer solid brick walls of the house are unusually thick. The windows are unusual in that they are five feet wide, and the front entrance is framed by a two columned portico. The house is surrounded by beautiful gardens and the circular brick driveway is bordered by boxwood.

ROSEDOWN

St. Francisville • Louisiana • 1835

Again, the Doric style of Greek architecture is used at Rosedown, with magnificent results, ornamented with balustrades and columns on both first and second stories. The house also has wings built of brick which were covered with cement, and topped by the same balustrades as the house. Rosedown is surrounded by some of the finest gardens in the state of Louisiana. Paths radiate out through the azaleas and camellias, past gazebos, fountains, and marble statues of mythological creatures. Then one can stroll back up the magnificent alley of live oaks toward the house, and appreciate the full splendor of this magnificent estate. *Located east of St. Francisville on LA 10 and US 61.*

BALFOUR HOUSE

Vicksburg • Mississippi • 1836

The architecture of the Balfour House was heavily influenced by the Greek classical school, but the overall appearance of the facade gives a stronger impression that it is basically a house of the Federal period. The entablature that crowns the parapet, and the portico is impressive, to say the least. The portico is supported by four Corinthian columns, which are repeated at the entrance beneath it. This home was shelled repeatedly during the siege of Vicksburg, and a cannonball did great damage, but still the house survived. Emma Balfour also survived the siege, and wrote in detail in her diary about the horrors and deprivations of the siege.

OAK ALLEY

Vacherie • Louisiana • 1836

The original name of Oak Alley was Bon Sejour, meaning pleasant sojourn, and a magnificent "Allee" led from the levee to the house, under a canopy of spreading live oak trees. The riverboat captains that passed the town of Vacherie always refered to the location as the "Oak Alley" and that name persisted. The house has three dormers on each side and the roof is crowned by a belvedere. The central structure is surrounded by columns and wrought iron galleries on all four sides. A series of french doors, fitted with dark green shutters, open onto the galleries on both levels. *Located on LA 18, above Vacherie, Louisiana.*

OAKLAWN MANOR

Franklin • Louisiana • 1837

Oaklawn Manner is a massive replica of a greek temple, but it has been decorated with wrought iron balconies and broad fanlights over the doorways. Even on the third floor, a smaller version of the balcony is placed in front of the attic windows. There is a magnificent courtyard in the rear with a geometrically designed small pool and fountain. The house is surrounded by tremendous live oak trees, said to comprise the largest grove of its kind. An old brick pathway leads to the garden by way of a row of Tennessee Red Cedar trees. *Located east of Franklin, Louisiana on Irish Bend Road in Bayou Teche country.*

HOUMAS HOUSE

Burnside • Louisiana • 1840

Houmas House is probably one of the purest and finest examples of architecture in the United States - a true classic. The octagonal garconnieres (houses for the boys - "les garcons") are also unique and classic. The enclosed belvedere at the center of the roof enabled the owners to see which packet boats were coming down the river and who was working in the sugar cane fields. As in other early homes, the size of the exterior of the house did not necessarily dictate the size of the interior rooms. Those at Houmas house are smaller and have lower ceilings than you would expect, but nevertheless, they were spacious enough. *Located on the River Road just upriver from Burnside, Louisiana.*

ROWAN OAK

Oxford • Mississippi • 1840

Home of famous Mississippian, Nobel prize winning author, William Faulkner. It has been kept as it was during Faulkner's lifetime. A long alley of tall, stately cedar trees frames the two story portico at the entrance, adding to the stately aspect of the home. The general appearance of the house exudes the quiet gentility that is often noticed in Mississippi homes. Rowan Oak is now owned by the University of Mississippi, where Faulkner seminars are held periodically.

CEDAR GROVE

Vicksburg • Mississippi • 1840

Cedar Grove rests on one of the many "terraces" that climb upwards from the Mississippi River to the main street of Vicksburg. Because of its elevation, it presents a monumental image to the visitor looking up at it. The upstairs gallery and the entablature of the roof are supported by pure Doric columns, and the galleries are embellished with the wrought iron work that was so popular at the time. There is an interesting curved bay window in the wing to the left.

DEVEREUX

Natchez • Mississippi • 1840

Devereux is a very pure interpretation of Greek Revival architecture. A small square belvedere sits atop the peak of the roof. The six fluted Doric columns that support the entablature at the roof line on the front gallery are elegant, indeed. The central doors on both levels are recessed, and a small wrought iron balcony adds the finishing touch to the upper doors. The tall windows on the front gallery begin at the floor, so that when they are open, they provide considerable ventilation.

MELROSE

Natchez • Mississippi • 1845

Pure of line and simple in ornamentation of wrought iron, placed in strategic locations with no pretense of show, this home is a classic example of the early Greek style house of Natchez. There is some Georgian influence in the style of doors and windows. At this stage of the development of the plantation homes, we begin to see very large, high ceilinged rooms appear. Cotton was making money for the Natchez planters, and they were ready to purchase such adornments as black marble mantles and French gold-leafed mirrors.

CAMELLIA PLACE

Columbus • Mississippi • 1847

Camellia Place is an enormous mansion, built of large handmade bricks, twice the size and weight of bricks made today. The front two-story portico adds to the grandeur of this mansion, and the entablature is supported by four square columns. Inside, a spiral staircase winds gracefully up to the fourth floor observatory, the crowning majesty of the house. The stairway is unsupported above the first floor. The entrance hall, parlor, and dining room are adorned with woodwork of solid mahogany.

MADEWOOD

Napoleonville • Louisiana • 1848

Madewood was designed using the second, or Ionic, phase of Greek Revival architecture. The mansion appears to be a grand temple, with fluted Ionic columns and a wing on either side of the main house, each of which looks like another temple in miniature. Instead of the traditional Palladian fanlight above the entablature, a fan motif has been carved into the wood. There is a winding staircase of walnut that travels the 25 foot distance to the second floor, and an enormous ballroom takes up a large portion of the space on the first floor. *Located on Bayou Lafourche near Napoleonville, Louisiana.*

WAVERLEY

West Point • Mississippi • 1852

Stories about Waverley tell us that the original owners were accustomed to luxury and extravagance to a fault. The architecture of the house seems to confirm the stories, for the design, both inside and out, is more than extravagant. On the interior, two matching curved staircases arise from two sides of the central hall, to meet again on the second floor, and then repeat this design again and yet again to the octagonal cupola on the fourth floor. From the connecting landing on each floor, a balcony completely encircles that floor, leaving an opening in the center of the house that rises all the way to the cupola at the top of the house. The Greek architecture here has moved into the Ionic phase. *Located in West Point, Mississippi - MS 50, north of Columbus.*

LANSDOWNE

Natchez • Mississippi • 1853

In the middle of the nineteenth century, we sometimes find houses that seem small and are referred to as "cottages," but we realize that we have been misled when we enter the home. The rooms are far more spacious than in some of the earlier, larger homes we have already seen. The architecture at Landsdowne is marvelous for its attention to detail. Fluted Doric columns are repeated in the door frame at the entrance, and a tiny semicircular window is placed in the triangle of the pediment. A delicately designed belvedere rests atop the roof like an ornament, and is guarded by a lacy balustrade.

SUNNYSIDE

Columbus • Mississippi • 1854

Sunnyside is one of many unusual antebellum homes that are found in Columbus, Mississippi. Some show a certain Greek revival influence, but the main characteristic of most of them is the unusual carpentry work that decorates the facade of the house. Sunnyside is no exception. The slender double colonnettes and the intricate woodwork of the balustrades shows magnificent detail work. This lovely home is framed by a beautifully landscaped lawn and tall shade trees.

TEZCUCO PLANTATION

Burnside • Louisiana • 1855

This house with the Aztec name was built by a family who had holdings in Mexico, and was named for the original city where Mexico City was founded. It is called a "raised cottage", although the ceilings are 15 feet high and some of the rooms are 25 feet square. It has the large expanse of roof, the galleries all around, and the tall louvred windows which kept a plantation house cool. The framing of the side galleries and the front gallery railings are all done in wrought iron of the grapevine design. The roof extension over the front gallery is supported by six large square columns. *Located on LA 44 downriver from Burnside, Louisiana.*

SAN FRANCISCO

Reserve • Louisiana • 1856

The inspiration for the architecture of San Francisco was based on the Gothic architecture of the river boats. One old-time river boatman called the fancy paddlewheeler boat an engine with a raft surrounded by thousands of dollars of jigsaw work around it. Nevertheless, this house is spectacular, and is furnished with grand antiques and elegant silk and tasseled draperies. The building is actually a galleried house in the old Creole style, with the main living quarters built over a raised basement, giving space for the various service rooms on the ground floor level. *Located on LA 44, 35 miles upriver from New Orleans, near Reserve, Louisiana.*

DUNLEITH

Natchez • Mississippi • 1856

Dunleith is similar to other plantations in Louisiana and Mississippi, but much grander in scale. The columns completely surround this mansion, giving it the peristyle aspect of a Greek temple. They are extremely tall, and support galleries at the second level on each side of the house. All of the windows continue down to the floor and are flanked by shutters (never called jalousies in Mississippi). The beautifully designed dormers and the tall chimneys call attention to the height of the roof, and the dentation trim of the pediment is exceptionally fine.

STANTON HALL

Natchez • Mississippi • 1857

Stanton Hall was built on the crest of a hill in the center of a city block in downtown Natchez. It is undoubtedly one of the grandest homes in the country. Granite steps lead up the front of this full blown example of Greek Revival architecture. It is adorned by front and side galleries, which are trimmed in lacy cast iron railings. Four fluted columns adorn the entrance and, although they are as ornate as Corinthian columns, they show the influence of Egyptian architecture. The interior of the house is as grand as the exterior, with double parlors, and a long dining room, lighted by wrought iron chandeliers that depict Indians, corn, fruit, animals and every imaginable thing that could be intricately intertwined in them .

NOTTOWAY

White Castle • Louisiana • 1857

Nottoway is believed to be the largest of the existing true southern plantation homes. It was built on a grand scale by John Hampton Randolph of the Virginia Randolphs. The elegant, curving front staircase and tall square columns add to the illusion of great height. The only word that describes it is palatial. A rounded wing on the upriver side of the house contains the famous white ballroom. Another wing at the rear forms an ell with the house and provides kitchen and work areas on the first floor, and extra bedrooms upstairs. *Located on the River Road on the west bank near White Castle, Louisiana.*

MERREHOPE

Meridian • Mississippi • 1858

Merrehope is a twenty room mansion of masterful style. Nine fluted Ionic columns support the roof, which extends out over the second floor gallery. The galleries are enclosed by an intricately designed balustrade that reminds us of the harem screens of the mideast. This moorish influence is often referred to as Islamic revival. The portico that protects the two-story bay has the unique shape of half an octagon, and graceful brackets support the eaves. The interior is beautifully ornamented with plaster medallions and cornices on the ceilings.

MAGNOLIA HALL

Natchez • Mississippi • 1858

Magnolia Hall is another mansion designed in the Ionic order of Classic Greek architecture employed in the mid nineteenth century. Four Ionic columns are tied together by the wooden balustrade. Soft brown colors of the house provide a relief from the parade of all white, or white and red brick homes. Magnolia Hall is located in downtown Natchez, not too far from the river, and it was shelled during the Civil War, but happily survived. It is now a combination of well furnished rooms and museum displays, featuring costumes of the Antebellum era.

LONGWOOD

Natchez • Mississippi • 1858 • 1861

In the architecture of Longwood, we see the peak of antebellum architecture, just before the Civil War, or the War between the States as it is often referred to in the South. Longwood was never finished because many of the carpenters were from the North, and when War broke out in 1861, the Yankee men packed up their tools and headed for home. Some of the tools still lie where they were left behind. In this octagonal edifice we see the extreme variety of fluted Corinthian columns topped by the beginnings of Victorian "Carpenter Gothic." Some of the arches are reminiscent of Moorish architecture that was introduced into Spain in earlier days. The onion dome complements this. Dr. Haller Nutt built the house, and it was known as "Nutt's Folly," but it is magnificent to behold.

SHADOWLAWN

Columbus • Mississippi • 1860

Shadowlawn combines Greek and Gothic details. This stately two story mansion, built of hand-hewn walnut and heart-pine, is actually in the Greek Revival style, but the front portico is framed by six columns of unusual style; arches between them that show the moorish flavor again, and a balcony set underneath the second floor doorway, all done in intricate carpenter gothic fretwork and fluting. The effect is something like looking at a huge white wedding cake. The houses in Columbus are very different from those in Natchez, although they span a similar period in time. One can have a unique experience by visiting the pilgrimages in both cities and comparing them.

THE COLONNADE

Columbus • Mississippi • 1860

This tall and wide, two-storied mansion, has a white columned facade, crowned by a deep entablature supported by six slender square columns across the front. The first and second floor doorways are offset to the side of the house, and the upper one has its own ornate balcony. The framing of the door and windows on the first floor is done in grand style, with excellent woodwork and moldings. Azaleas and white dogwood adorn the yard. This is the last home in the book of the so-called "Antebellum houses" (meaning "before the war").

THE JOSEPH JEFFERSON WINTER HOME

Delcambre • Louisiana • 1870

This is one of the later historic homes of the 19th Century and is decorated with wonderful gingerbread trim. Porches and gables project from every side; and from the observatory at the top, one can see for miles over the flat surrounding countryside. It was set on top of a salt dome and is flanked by historic live oak trees and the famous Live Oak Gardens. Joe Jefferson was the actor who became famous for his role as Rip Van Winkle. The interior rooms of the house are charming, and are in keeping with the Victorian style of decoration. *Located at Jefferson Island near Delcambre, not far from New Iberia.*

FIDDLER'S FOLLY

Oxford • Mississippi • 1875

Fiddler's Folly is unique among early Victorian homes. The central portion, of pleasing design with peaked roof, is flanked by twin porches on both levels. The original owner had the ingenuity to order one of the nations earlier prefabricated frame houses, but it was done on a grand scale. The home was designed and partially fabricated in England and the precut parts were then shipped to Oxford and assembled there. The same architects are said to have designed the Savoy Hotel in London. The facade of this home is so intricately styled and so charming, it is difficult to imagine it was a prefabricated structure.

WOLF-SCHLESINGER HOUSE

St. Francisville • Louisiana • 1880

The Wolf-Schlesinger House is as fine an example of Victorian architectures that can be found, and shows the strong Gothic influence that prevailed at the time it was built. The tall gables with their steep roofs, with a miniature gable set between them are literally covered with that jigsawed woodwork that we now refer to as gingerbread. A long veranda, supported by slender columns, extends along the front. An overhanging roof shades floor to ceiling windows framed in more detailed woodwork. This house is now being used as the St. Francisville Inn.

VICTORIA

Aberdeen • Mississippi • 1885

Victoria is appropriately named, because it has a very Victorian look about it. The twin gables, each with its high peaked roof, little round window, and vertical paneling are charming. The left one sits atop a lovely bay window, and the right side of the home has a shaded porch with slender columns and modified arches in between. The house is partially hidden behind a dignified brick wall with piers and gate. Victoria is well worth a trip to Aberdeen, just to view the exterior of this pretty little invention.

F.W. WILLIAMS HOUSE

Meridian • Mississippi • 1886

In the Frank W. Williams House we see the epitome of pure Victorian architecture, devoid of gingerbread or embellishment of any sort. A row of slender, pencil thin posts support the overhanging porch roof. A cleverly designed extension of the corner of the porch, having its own gable, adds distinction to the house. The roof is a mountain of gables, all intricately fitted together. The front and center gable is a typically Victorian inverted V, and two other gables extend out on both sides of the main roof. A long narrow ventilator in the front gable has the shape of a Gothic window.

GLENCOE

Wilson • Louisiana • 1897

A true Victorian castle, Glencoe is the epitome of the grandiose "American architecture" of the period, complete with towers and turrets and gables, and enormous in size. It is a collection of architectural delights typical of Queen Anne Victorian. First and second floor galleries continue in and out across the various protrusions and insets, all guarded by balustrades.

Finished in beaded wood, the dining room presents a unique feature. All of the pieces of beading were kept in order as they came out of the lumber mill, so that the wood grain is continuous throughout the beaded paneling on the walls of the room - most unusual. *Located north of Jackson, Louisiana at Wilson on Hwy 19.*

GREENWOOD - A RECONSTRUCTION

St. Francisville • Louisiana • 1830 • 1968

The original Greenwood Plantation was built in 1830 and was a splendid creation indeed. Tall and stately, with twenty eight pristine white Doric columns encircling the house, it is a breathtaking experience to come upon it in the midst of a grove of trees. All of us who remember it can still recall its reflection in the lake at the base of the sloping hill on which it stood. The roof was completely hidden by the sumptuous wide cornice that was supported by the columns.

It seemed that the end had come when Greenwood tragically burned to the ground in 1960, but the twenty eight stately columns remained standing like ghosts of the past. The Barnes family miraculously restored the entire home after they purchased it in 1968, and it has regained all of its original grandeur. This was truly a labor of love, and the reflection has returned to the lake. *Located North of St. Francisville, Louisiana, off the Angola Road, leading from US 61.*

Cistern at San Francisco
Reserve, Louisiana

Photo by Bobby Potts

Cistern at Bocage
Burnside, Louisisana

Photo by Ed Minvielle

Well House at Hermitage
Darrow, Louisiana

Photo by Ed Minvielle

Gazebo at Rosedown
St. Francisville, Louisiana

Photo by Ed Minvielle

DECORATIVE ADDITIONS TO THE ESTATES

Gazebos • Wells Houses • Cisterns

The decorative additions to the plantation grounds were also useful. Rainwater was collected from the wide gutters that encircled the roof. From there it then ran through a pipe into the cistern, which was often just a plain wooden tank. Sometimes a fancy top was added, as with the cisterns at San Francisco. At Bocage, the cisterns were hidden in replicas of gun powder houses, more in the style of Williamsburg than Louisiana, but clever. The well houses added an attractive cover to the well, and the gazebos provided cool shady places to sit.

Kitchen wing and upstairs
bedrooms at Nottoway
White Castle, Louisiana

Photo by Bobby Potts

**Garconniere at
Houmas House
Burnside, Louisiana**

Photo by Bobby Potts

**Kitchen garden at
Acadian House
St. Martinville, Louisiana**

Photo by Ed Minvielle

SERVICE AREAS

Of Plantation Homes

This book would not be complete without mentioning some of the working areas that were an integral part of the old plantations. Kitchens were often in separate areas, either in a wing in the rear, or in a separate building. The reason for this was the danger of fire, and also the heat that would be added to the living area, which one did not need in a hot climate. There was always a kitchen garden, which served the kitchen with vegetables, herbs, and seasonings - particularly the hot red peppers. The upper part of the wing often provided extra bedrooms, or a separate house was built for the boys and young men of the house. Since the French word for boy is "garcon," these separate buildings were called "garconnieres."

Dairy House at Auburn
Natchez, Mississippi

Photo by Ed Minvielle

Pigeonniere in
Baton Rouge, Louisiana

Photo by Bobby Potts

Sykes Barn in
Aberdeen, Mississippi

Photo by Bobby Potts

OUTBUILDINGS

Of Plantation Homes

These buildings are all connected with the production of food for the plantation: milk, squab, and beef. Plantation people ate well, and raised a great variety of food products for those who lived and worked on the plantation. The pigeonnieres were the French version of the English dove cotes.

IN MEMORIAM

Many wonderful plantation houses have been lost during the last fifty years. They are sorely missed by those of us who fondly remember them. Hopefully, those that remain will be preserved for our children to see. Below is a list of some of the many that have disappeared, with the cause of their disappearance:

• • • • • • • • • • •

Afton Villa Plantation, St. Francisville, La. - fire

Belle Chasse Plantation, Belle Chasse, La. - demolition

Belle Grove Plantation, Donaldsonville, La. - neglect and fire

Belmont Plantation, Grosse Tete, La. - neglect

The Cottage Plantation, Baton Rouge, La. - fire

Elmwood Plantation, Destrehan, La. - fire

Fairview Plantation, St. Francisville - fire

Greenwood Plantation (original), St. Francesville, La. - fire

Linwood Plantation, Dutchtown, La. - fire

Mt. Airey Plantation, Reserve, La. - demolition

Seven Oaks Plantation, Westwego, La. - neglect

Trepagnier Plantation, Destrehan, La. - neglect

Uncle Sam Plantation, Convent, La. - demolition

Valcour Aime Plantation, St. James, La. - neglect

Versailles Plantation, Chalmette, La. - neglect

Welham Plantation, College Point, La. - demolition

White Hall Plantation - Union, La. - neglect

Woodlawn Plantation, Napoleonville, La. - neglect

Zenon Trudeau House - Convent, La. - neglect

• • • • • • • • • • •

There are undoubtly many more that have been lost, of which I do not have information. Natchez seems to have a better record of saving houses, probably because of its early interest in the pilgrimage.

In Louisiana, many that were in pitiful condition were saved in the nick of time by people who cared enough to restore them. Just simple maintenance on these large homes is costly, and owners are to be congratulated for their efforts.

AFTON VILLA GARDENS

St. Francisville • Louisiana • 1849 - 1963

The marvelous gardens are all that remains of Afton Villa. It was built in 1849, incorporating a 1790 pioneer house and forty rooms. It was an English Manor house. However, it was built by a French architect and was an eclectic copy of a French Villa, incorporating all of the Gothic embellishments that were introduced in the early Victorian era. The house was destroyed by fire in 1963. *Located in St. Francisville, Louisiana, Hwy 61 North.*

• • • • • • • • • • •

PHOTOGRAPHY

Front Cover © Dick Dietrich, Page 1 © (Far Left) Bobby Potts, Page 1 (Middle Right) © Bobby Potts, Page 1 © (Far Right) © Ken Raveill, Page 2 © Bobby Potts, Page 3 © Bobby Potts, Page 4 © Bobby Potts, Page 5 © Bobby Potts, Page 6 © Ken Raveill, Page 7 © Bobby Potts, Page 8 © Ken Raveill, Page 9 © Bobby Potts, Page 10 © Bobby Potts, Page 11 © Bobby Potts, Page 12 © Ken Raveill, Page 13 © Bobby Potts, Page 14 © Ken Raveill, Page 15 © Ken Raveill, Page 16 © Bobby Potts, Page 17 © Ken Raveill, Page 18 © Bobby Potts, Page 19 © Ken Raveill, Page 20 © Bobby Potts, Page 21 © Ken Raveill, Page 22 © Ken Raveill, Page 23 © Ken Miquez, Page 24 © Dick Dietrich, Page 25 © Ken Raveill, Page 26 © Ken Raveill, Page 27 © Tom Till, Page 28 © Ken Raveill, Page 29 © Bobby Potts, Page 30 © Dick Dietrich, Page 31 © Ken Raveill, Page 32 © Clemenz Photography, Page 33 © Dick Dietrich, Page 34 © Dick Dietrich, Page 35 © Ken Raveill, Page 36 © Ken Raveill, Page 37 © Monserrate J. Schwartz, Page 38 © Ken Raveill, Page 39 © Ken Raveill, Page 40 © Ken Raveill, Page 41 © Ken Raveill, Page 42 © Ken Raveill, Page 43 © Ken Raveill, Page 44 © Ken Raveill, Page 45 © Dick Dietrich, Page 46 © Ken Raveill, Page 47 © Dick Dietrich, Page 48 © Ken Raveill, Page 49 © Ken Raveill, Page 50 © Ken Raveill, Page 51 © Bobby Potts, Page 52 © Ken Raveill, Page 53 © Ken Raveill, Page 54 © Bobby Potts, Page 55 © Bobby Potts, Page 56 © Ken Raveill, Page 57 © Bobby Potts, Page 58 © Bobby Potts, Page 59 © Ken Raveill, Page 60 © Ken Raveill, Back Cover © Ken Raveill.

ORDER FORM

If you would like to order additional copies of this book or sample some of our other fine products, please fill out the form below and mail to:

YOUR POINT OF PURCHASE RETAILER
OR
R.A.L. ENTERPRISES
Suite 136, 5000 A West Esplande Ave. • Metaire, LA 70006

TITLE		COST	QUANTITY	TOTAL
HISTORIC HOUSES OF THE DEEP SOUTH	64 pgs.	$12.95		
Cookin' Country Cajun (Hard Cover)	64 pgs.	$9.95		
Cookin' Country Cajun (Soft Cover)	64 pgs.	$7.95		
Cookin' on the Mississippi (Hard Cover)	64 pgs.	$9.95		
Cookin' on the Mississippi (Soft Cover)	64 pgs.	$7.95		
Favorite Recipes from New Orleans	64 pgs.	$7.95		
Southern Seafood Sampler	64 pgs.	$7.95		
Favorite Drinks of New Orleans	32 pgs.	$4.95		
Plantation Country Guide	64 pgs.	$7.95		
New Orleans - Birthplace of Jazz	56 pgs.	$7.95		
New Orleans - Crescent City	32 pgs.	$4.95		
Laminated New Orleans Placemats	Set of 4	$9.95		
Laminated Louisiana Plantation Placemats	Set of 4	$9.95		
Laminated Mississippi Plantation Placemats	Set of 4	$9.95		
New Orleans Coloring Book	32 pgs.	$4.95		
Louisiana / Mississippi Coloring Book	32 pgs.	$4.95		
Recipe Box Cards	Set of 10	$5.95		
			Postage & Handling	$2.00
			TOTAL	

☐ Check Enclosed ☐ Visa ☐ MasterCard ☐ American Express ☐ Discover

Card Number________________ Expiration Date ________

Name ________________________

Address ______________________

City______________ State ______ Zip ______

Daytime Phone (   ) __________________

All items are satisfaction guaranteed and your purchase will be promtly refunded if returned within 30 days.
Please allow two-four weeks for delivery. No foreign orders please.

ORDER FORM

If you would like to order additional copies of this book or sample some of our other fine products, please fill out the form below and mail to:

YOUR POINT OF PURCHASE RETAILER
OR
R.A.L. ENTERPRISES
Suite 136, 5000 A West Esplande Ave. • Metaire, LA 70006

TITLE		COST	QUANTITY	TOTAL
HISTORIC HOUSES OF THE DEEP SOUTH	64 pgs.	$12.95		
Cookin' Country Cajun (Hard Cover)	64 pgs.	$9.95		
Cookin' Country Cajun (Soft Cover)	64 pgs.	$7.95		
Cookin' on the Mississippi (Hard Cover)	64 pgs.	$9.95		
Cookin' on the Mississippi (Soft Cover)	64 pgs.	$7.95		
Favorite Recipes from New Orleans	64 pgs.	$7.95		
Southern Seafood Sampler	64 pgs.	$7.95		
Favorite Drinks of New Orleans	32 pgs.	$4.95		
Plantation Country Guide	64 pgs.	$7.95		
New Orleans - Birthplace of Jazz	56 pgs.	$7.95		
New Orleans - Crescent City	32 pgs.	$4.95		
Laminated New Orleans Placemats	Set of 4	$9.95		
Laminated Louisiana Plantation Placemats	Set of 4	$9.95		
Laminated Mississippi Plantation Placemats	Set of 4	$9.95		
New Orleans Coloring Book	32 pgs.	$4.95		
Louisiana / Mississippi Coloring Book	32 pgs.	$4.95		
Recipe Box Cards	Set of 10	$5.95		
			Postage & Handling	$2.00
			TOTAL	

☐ Check Enclosed ☐ Visa ☐ MasterCard ☐ American Express ☐ Discover

Card Number________________ Expiration Date ________

Name ________________________

Address ______________________

City______________ State ______ Zip ______

Daytime Phone (   ) __________________

All items are satisfaction guaranteed and your purchase will be promtly refunded if returned within 30 days.
Please allow two-four weeks for delivery. No foreign orders please.